Manifesting Holistic Health Through Diversity Worldwide

Jo Sonsè, BS, CMT, HBMT è

Manifesting Holistic Health Through Diversity Worldwide
Copyright ©2017 Jo Sonsè. All rights reserved.

No part of this book may be reproduced in any form or by any mechanical means, including information storage and retrieval systems without permission in writing from the publisher/author, except by a reviewer who may quote passages in a review.

All images, logos, quotes, and trademarks included in this book are subject to use according to trademark and copyright laws of the United States of America.

Sonsè, Jo, Author
Manifesting Holistic Health Through Diversity Worldwide
Jo Sonsè

ISBN: 978-1976302251

SELF HELP

QUANTITY PURCHASES: Schools, companies, professional groups, clubs, and other organizations may qualify for special terms when ordering quantities of this title. For information, email btbjson@gmail.com

This book is printed in the United States of America.

Other books written by the author:

"Massaging in Times of Illness: My Experience with Massage for Breast Cancer and HIV/AIDS",

Reaching for Recovery and Wellness with Benefits from Massage: Experiences of People with Mental Health Issues".

EMDR Project "Remote Control: A Healer's Journey thru Open Wounds to Soft Scars".

This book is dedicated to:

Crista Keller, MD

Holly Vause, DNP, PMHNP-BC

Kseniya Bakhtin, MA, NCC, LPC

Preface

Jo Sonsé has been a friend of mine for five years. I have spent a
substantial amount of time with her which has allowed me to learn much
about her.

Jo's father was in the U.S. Air Force thus allowing Jo to live abroad. Her
name, Sonsé I obviously French. Anyone who is bi-lingual is
automatically impressive to me since I spent thirty years on the Mexican
border and studied Opera with language dictation in that part of the
country.

It is obvious to me that from day one, Jo did everything in her youth to
prepare for Professional Physical Education. She has a Bachelor's of
Science degree in Physical Education and is formally trained with
Certifications in general and specialized massage therapy. I have two
years of steady experience benefiting from both areas of her training. She
has trained me in the proper and safe methods of physical conditioning.
She was sensitive to my advanced age and kept me from injuring myself
during this time. The one time that I did injury myself during this same
time was when I listened to someone else in the same department. Jo's
healing techniques in massage, she was able to minimize my pain and
discomfort due to the injury in my back.

I miss my weekly visits to her in those two years. Whenever I would go to
these sessions, her chair massages would put me into the mental and

physical zone. Her compassion and tenderness alone with her wonderful recordings of ambient music and the darkness of the room, was healing to me during this difficult time in my life.

Sometimes we wouldn't talk at all during these sessions. Other times, we would have soothing conversation. In some ways, it reminded me of all the years that I went to the same barber and always left not only being groomed but mentally uplifted. After those first two years, I became personal friends with Jo Sonsè'. She has been generous with her time and helped me financially, when I was sick and unable to do the occasional odd jobs to generate a supplemental income for myself.

I have been an independent contractor all my working life. I bring this up because entrepreneurs are always looking for associates to be loyal team players who would have to be on their backs before they would let you down. This valuable trait describes my friend, Jo.

There's much more that I could tell you about my friend, Jo. Perhaps I should write a book!

Louis Bell, Self-Employed Contractor
Professional Musician

Table of Contents

"For I know the plans I have for you," declared the Lord, "Plans to prosper you & not to harm you. Plans to give you Hope & a Future."

Jeremiah 29:11

Introduction

A definition for "Holistic Lifestyles" I found on the Internet reads: "A lifestyle which makes you feel like a complete person through your health, relationships, financial, spiritual connections, and the ability to create and heal."

In this book, I want to take a look at all these areas and share my perspectives on how to make it possible for us to all work together in sustaining and maintaining Holistic Health. I will be using my experiences in Denver, Colorado, but really see it as a microcosm for many other cities throughout the world who experience homelessness, poverty, mental illness, diverse populations, medical centers and non-traditional healing centers.

While I know no city or country is exactly alike, we will simply be looking at my unique experience in the Greater Denver area, outlying suburbs, and rural populations that I have worked with. Some chapters may seem like an unlikely topic in relationship to Holistic Health, but I hope to clear any confusion and offer a unique blend of visionary ideas to bring them all together.

"It takes a common vision to raise a child,

It takes a common vision to raise a book,

I thank the voices

From the past, the Sight from the future

The Wisdom from the now."

        Dorothy May

Chapter 1: Spiritual Connections

"When we humbly pray that God/Spirit would give unbelievers life and ask God/Spirit to send a messenger, we shouldn't be surprised to find out later that we are the messengers God had in mind. In fact, those who have a personal prayer life with God have probably been the messengers whom God has sent in response to other people's prayers."

    Neil T. Anderson

A lot of people think medicine is first, and I feel spirituality is first in a person's life to bring holistic health. My Spiritual journey right now has me attending Highlands Church in Denver, Colorado. Highlands is the first church where I have felt inclusiveness within my spiritual life. I have been attending since February 2017. Every Sunday we are greeted with the church Ethos before the sermon starts. It is:

"Married, divorced and single here,
It's one family that mingles here.
Conservative and liberal here,
We've all gotta give a little here.
Big and small here,
There's room for us all here.
Doubt and belief here,
We all can receive here.
LGBTQ and straight here,
There's no hate here.

Woman and man here,

Everyone can here.

Whatever your race here,

For all of us grace here.

In imitation of the ridiculous love Almighty God has for each of us and all
of us,

Let us live and love without labels!"

    Mark Tidd

To me, this statement makes people of a wide diversity feel completely
accepted. Highlands Church intends to grow into other areas of Colorado
and eventually out of State to spread this message of inclusion. I am
greeted as I enter the church and find fellowship with people in my row,
the next row, and my involvement.

It's amazing to me the diversity sitting in this church located within a
former theatre. And the Ethos isn't just lip service, it truly is what is says
at each opening sermon. Bible based, we have ministers come from other
churches to give the sermon. I'm trying to find where I fit with the church
as far as what else I want to participate in as a lay person. I'm not in any
rush as I want to grow with the church progressively.

I feel Spirit, Mother Earth and the Holy Spirit are embedded in my core
and have been since childhood. I felt this connection not in church
buildings, and not in the Catholic Church that I was raised in, but as a
spiritual practice every night before bed and in my friendships.

The first church I ever felt connection with people was the Metropolitan Community Church of Denver (MCC) in 1989. It was, and probably still is, an LGBT-friendly church in Denver. I became the Property Manager and Event Coordinator there. Several of us we able to convert a large room in the church into a food bank. Our maintenance man built a closet specifically for keeping the food that was donated. We totally revamped the room with new paint, lighting, and carpet and added a new, secure door. We were also able to put in a movable wall that opened between the sanctuary and the social hall after church service and renovated the bathrooms. All this happened within a period of 3 months. It was phenomenal for me to see how well we all worked together and how Spirit moves in special ways.

Working with gay men again also brought me a ton of healing. I was the only woman and only lesbian on the team and it had not been my experience in the past that men were comfortable being supervised or directed by me, but this time was different. Not only did we work collaboratively to achieve so much, I also received healing from them not passing away. That may sound funny, but I had many gay men with AIDS who saw me for massage and they passed away. Now I was able to work with gay men without losing them, and that was healing.

When I was at MCC, Nancy Keene included me in Soul Force which was and is a movement to have LGBTQ recognized not only in Episcopalian Churches, but also Catholic and Presbyterian ones, including supporting

LGBTQ marriages. As part of Soul Force, we performed a non-violent protest against the Episcopalian Church who were holding their National Conference in Denver. The Episcopalian Churches at that the time weren't accepting of gay marriages, and we felt the protest would make a big impact because Al Gore was the Vice President of the Conference and was going to be in attendance. We locked arms and wouldn't let people enter the Convention Center. Our protest was the first in the country in support of LGBTQ marriage legalization and equality.

The police arrested us, put us in buses, and locked us up two by two. It was an amazing experience and was the first major act of civil disobedience I've done. The police said we were the most non-violent protest they ever experienced. We made all the newspapers, especially in conservative Colorado Springs. I clipped every paper I could and made an entire album of the event. Being both gay and Christian is important to me. It means I can live the fullest of my truth. I will stand behind gay brothers and sisters to show support and fight for equal rights.

Shortly after this experience, I decided to attend Johnson & Wales (Culinary) University to build my skills. I was introduced to the "Course in Miracles", and while most people go through it in a group setting, with being a full-time student, I developed my own private spiritual practice by going through it on my own. I read every night for a year and it really helped me rekindle my inner passion for massage. At the time, I was still doing massage but the love I had felt for the people I worked on just wasn't there. The Course in Miracles had a profound effect on me. It is mostly a right brain book, but reading it will change you even if you aren't right brained.

So, I was doing massage and began working with food after my training at Johnson & Wales. The Course in Miracles re-ignited my passion, which I feel put love back into my hands. With both food and massage, I use my hands and really try to use my love and infuse that into everything I touch. In fact, I make bread for my friends and they ask for the recipe, but when they make it, it doesn't taste the same. I truly believe it is because of the extra ingredient of love.

At this time I am planning on writing a cookbook.

I was later to meet Emily Fitz-Randolph who is a guiding light in my life, and joined her church, who I won't identify. I didn't know at the time they were not supportive of gays, however, fellowship was the most important aspect of attending for me, and after 2 total knee replacements, the congregation brought me a meal every other day after having surgery, for two months. I was touched by this act. I was so thankful that after recovery, I started bring meals to families with newborns. I also joined my first prayer circle once a week with church. It gave me time to be with the Pastor and Deacon and talked about what was holding us back, and to pray for different issues, locally and globally. I was able to bring my spirituality deep into my core. Before then, my experience was only with Mother Earth, and with this I was able to really feel Jesus and it was more personable to have such a small group to do this with. From that I was also able to give massage to the Pastor, which was a new experience for me. I was able to love him as a man but not a pastor due to his beliefs against gays. I also went on to massage his family members even after I left his church. He said he knew the Lord worked through my hands- he still supported me even though we disagreed.

I even feel my connection with my dog Diamond was also a spiritual connection. The first time I saw Diamond he was 12 weeks old and living at the Dumb Friends League. He had a white light around him and I knew we would grow older together because Spirit was within and around him.

Many times when felt I had nothing else in my life, I definitely felt Mother Earth working through me and for me. When we feel we have nothing else, Spirit is always there. While in the Catholic Church, I used the word, "God", but wasn't one for adoring buildings or priests. Today, I use Spirit, Mother Earth and Holy Spirit.

"Did you know that massage is one of the oldest and simplest forms of healthcare? It is depicted in Egyptian tomb paintings. It is mentioned in ancient Chinese, Japanese and Indian texts. In 5 B.C. the Greek physician Hippocrates said the secret to health was a good oil massage."

    -Anonymous quote

While I was at the Boulder College of Massage Therapy, my focus and my internships were with Breast Cancer and HIV/AIDS organizations. I volunteered at running road races and walks focusing on the two illnesses as well.

I chose to work with breast cancer patients because a woman I knew who was influential in my life was diagnosed with it. I also learned lesbians have the highest risk of breast cancer due to the fact most of them do not bear children- a known risk factor. This made it even more dear to me. I also felt HIV/AIDS patients were a greatly underserved population that honestly a lot of people were scared to work with for fear of contracting the disease. While other students brought in a lot of physical therapy types of clients, I focused all my training massages on these two populations.

After graduating, I went to work at Colorado University Health Science Center (CUHSC) and immediately started massaging HIV/AIDS clients – both men and women. I also began getting clients from University Hospital who had breast cancer. I talked to my massage supervisor about my client focus and she created a course for Hospital Based Massage Therapy. There were six of us who studied through experiential clients at the hospital, while under supervision. She requested the Colorado School of Healing Arts create a certificate program and after 6 months we each received certification and could be paid for our services. I worked within the Oncology, Bone Marrow, and HIV/AIDS units.

During that time, I would get a call that a patient in the Bone Marrow Transplant Unit (now called Stem Cell Research) wanted a 20 minute massage. Within a hospital setting, a 20 minute session was the most I would provide, and would massage women from all over the world. University Hospital is a research and teaching hospital, so they had a wide variety of patients. I was taught more about the medical components of, and the effects on the body of the patient's illnesses. I began providing Hospital Based Massage Therapy to other Denver hospitals as well when some of my clients were admitted there. It was a tremendous experience that opened up to
UCHSC massage therapists afterwards, although the program ended in 2000. Hospital Based Massage Therapy was delegated to nurses, who weren't happy with the change as they already had their hands full with other tasks. My role then became training those going through their Master's in Nursing on massage. Again, without formal training or curriculum, this too has gone by the wayside.

Soon after, I created and led a large massage-a-thon for breast cancer and HIV/AIDS at CUHSC. We had 40 massage therapists and held 180 appointments in a doctor's multidisciplinary setting. We learned so much, but unfortunately, I realized too late that I should have performed research studies. I had performed a research project in massage school and my instructor encouraged me to continue doing so.

In 2001, I went to Mental Health Center of Denver (MHCD) 2Succeed Program and started massaging people with mental health issues. There I would massage each patient 15 minutes once a week, and I did this for 13 years. I used my medical experience to work on people with a variety of issues, not only mental diagnoses. The staff at 2Succeed had no idea the complexities involved with massaging people who were on various medications or the diverse side effects of those. I read voraciously about medications, diagnoses and side effects and came to the conclusion I would never massage a client longer than 15 minutes. Because of this, I would work on 24 patients in one day, each and every week.

Once again I realized after 13 years I could have done some really amazing research on mental health issues, diagnosis, medication, as well as massage's effect on resting pulse rate, blood pressure and other points of psychiatric and medical interest. I intend that wherever I land next in my career, I will definitely incorporate research in massage therapy.

"If we can muster up that degree of commitment and get away from the uniquely American perception that if something can't be done immediately it isn't worth doing, then I think the Hunger Movement, this small but growing minority of us, can have a truly significant impact."

Harry Chapin, singer/songwriter

I have a huge vision for a multi-disciplinary wellness center that I have shared with others, and want to share here with you as well. It is all about creating a center to assist people from low-income, poverty, and disabilities to move toward middle income/class and sustain self-sufficiency. The need for this type of center is huge and would demonstrate how people can start right where they are and move towards a higher standard of living. Foundationally, it would be a people first/business second model involving a pay-as-you can concept for services.

The components of the center include:

Café

Food Bank

Chair Massage

Art Room

Music Room

Fitness Center/ Well-being Program

Job Center/ Computer Lab

Service in Exchange for Rent Units

Café

Open 3 days per week, Tuesday, Thursday and Saturday, it would initially be ran by volunteers until grants, donations and sales could sustain employees and business expenses. As a pay-what-you-can café, patrons would either pay for their meals or donate time somewhere in the facility, or both. People unable to pay would be encouraged to work up to the ability to pay. Quarterly, the café could host fundraising dinners and the facilities could be rented to the public for additional income during non-working hours.

The awareness of 'free' anything always spreads fast. Low cost services are purchased more often, and in larger quantities, than luxury services/goods. When pricing isn't a barrier, more people buy (and share) according to the "Complete Guide to Pay What You Want Pricing: How You Can Share Your Work and Still Make a Profit", by Tom Morkes.

This model can show the power of generosity, even if you don't believe in it. The service will need to be promoted, but then will spread with word of mouth. Using staff's network of connections could be an easy way to begin this and get it out to the public. Purchasing needs to also be available on credit card as this usually causes people to pay more than cash does. Pay-what-you-can pricing helps people make creative, and positive changes in the life. Most cafés using this method find success, and we would incorporate it not only in the café but also in the rest of the Multi-Disciplinary Wellness Center.

Food Bank

Also open 3 days a week, (Monday, Wednesday and Friday), and volunteer led, the food bank would serve those able to prepare meals for themselves or others. The food bank could remain volunteer based or funds could be directed here through grants, donations or other Wellness Center revenues.

Chair Massage

Chair massage could be offered 2 days a week in two shifts, such as 10am-12:30pm and 1pm-3:30pm. Each massage would be 15 minutes in length and the clients remain fully clothed. This area could be staffed by area massage school students under a supervisor in order to gain training hours for graduation. Once again this would be supported by grants, donations and sales from the chair massage by those able to pay.

The Chair Massage Program in itself provides:

A sense of well-being,

Relieves anxiety,

Increases circulation,

Reduces muscle fatigue and tension,

Boosts your immune system and resistance to illness,

Lowers your blood pressure,

Relieves muscle pain and headaches,

Improves thinking and awareness,

Increases stamina and energy,

Improves sleep,

Encourages better posture,

Generates more flexibility,

Builds awareness of breathing and relaxing.

These points are taken from the American Massage Therapy Association

Art Room and Gallery

Self-expression is important and lost frequently in low income communities. Participants would have access to various means of expression and could offer their art in an attached gallery. Art could also be available for sale by being displayed throughout the center with contact details to allow for purchase. Rotating art displays would keep the gallery fresh and enticing and encourage more art.

Fitness Center/ Well-Being Program

The Well-Being Program would offer both equipment and classes. Elliptical machines, recumbent machines, treadmills, speed balls and gloves, and free weights can be obtained through donations. Classes such as aerobics, yoga, meditation and spirituality can be offered by both volunteers and paid staff funded by grants, donations and member fees.

Music Room

The center would feature a sound proof music room for members to make CDs and to perform around Denver area venues for a fee. Revenue generated from the sale of the CD's and from performances can go right back into the program.

Job Center/ Computer Lab

The job program would house computers for people to get GEDs, increase social media skills, take online courses, and create resumes.

Service in Exchange for Rent Housing

Four apartments would be designated for two property managers and two janitorial staff who would each work 20 hours per week, building up to 40 hours.

To begin we would need a team, including a Board of Directors, Advisory Council, Guest Facilitators, and Volunteers. There would be a Program Director, two Wellness Program Assistants, (my job would be an Assistant Program and Community Service Coordinator), and a specialist for each program plus a business office with staff. These jobs would all be paid an affordable pay scale. There would be a semi-circular desk for three or four reception stations. The people working the stations would greet people, answer phones, make reservations, transfer calls and take messages.

"Don't give up on something just because you can't do it."
Chanda Kohhar

The Benefits of the Multi-Disciplinary Wellness Center

The Center's objective is to provide job opportunities to homeless and low-income applicants. There would need to be a specialist for each program but opportunities will exist in each program to hire disadvantaged people. I realize homeless and low-income people have gaps in their resumes which likely has caused them to not be chosen for jobs in the past. This creates a cycle between being able to find an affordable home and having an address to claim. However, if we can demonstrate through the Wellness Center that low income and homeless people aren't lazy or "just not working hard enough", we can change perceptions.

From data I've looked at, 70% of homeless people in Washington DC experience discrimination yearly. It is why we want to hire disadvantaged people into the Wellness Center and challenge neighbors to see them working hard within an affordable neighborhood. A current example of this is Hirschfield Towers in the Baker Neighborhood in Denver as well as MHCD's 2Succeed. However, 2Succeed only hires people in the middle income bracket and some disabled people on SSI or SSDI, rather than homeless or poverty level.

The key to hiring homeless and disadvantaged people is in understanding they need support in the process from those who aren't disadvantaged and working. Homeless people in shelters do indeed have to work harder because they have to get in line for the shower, grab breakfast, and probably catch a bus to get to work. It takes a tremendous amount of work to get out of homelessness and it should be noted this is their circumstance to overcome. Don't get me wrong, this will take a huge learning curve for everyone, but everyone will grow through the process. The overall goal would be in offering transitional jobs that start at minimum wage and offer pay increases upon satisfactorily maintaining and doing their jobs, and ultimately being able to afford housing. Additionally, they would striving for a 40 hour work schedule either at the center or at another job they are qualified to obtain.

As a non-profit, I believe it will do remarkably well, creating enough revenue to continue to build and add programs year over year. The Center ideally would exist in an area where there is already affordable housing established and be on a bus-line. It would emphasize hiring different people of color, gender identities, sexual orientations, and ages. Job coaches, with the use of the job center, would oversee job training and education for both staff and clients. Specialists and the Director would provide social and emotional support to disadvantaged employees and volunteers until it is determined who could best provide this service. It's important to have a healthy living, and safe neighborhood where the Center is located, with it being key for involvement by the Neighborhood Association.

Our café and volunteer-run food bank would provide nutritious food for those in critical need of food support while the other programs would be providing education within the programs listed. It would be good to have fundraisers such as at a Top Chef Competition in Denver at the café.

Chapter 4: Educational Visions

I've been performing chair massages for the Women's Homelessness Initiative for 2 years (2015-2017). And I will continue until women are no longer homeless! Did you ever see the movie "Pay It Forward"? Well, it's part of my life to gift the homeless women of Denver. Because I have been homeless twice, I wanted to give back to a community I had been part of. I also want to bring attention to homeless women, and I didn't feel there were many resources in 1999. This Saturday, as I do once a month, I will massage about 25 women who meet at a specific bus stop to come and get a meal and a chair massage. It's an important part of my practice.

These are women who are a little rough around the edges, and their energy levels are low. Many of them have been abused on the streets, suffer from depression, and dealing with things the average person who would come in for a massage aren't facing. I never know what it's going to be like for them- if they've been beaten, they could be bleeding, have ribs outs, or painful bruising. I have to be tender and they have to be willing to trust me. However, after even just a 15 minute chair massage, they become so grounded it takes them awhile to leave because they aren't used to someone touching them kindly or with care.

This is not a memoir of my childhood, but I want to share a bit about the lack of support I had when I became homeless. It taught me a lot about my intrinsic worth and the strange, unusual supports that got me back on my feet, stabilized, and forging my way back into life. In fact, the greatest educational experiences I ever had were 1) overcoming from homelessness in 1971 when I was 17 years of age and 2) overcoming homelessness again in 1998 when I was 44 years of age. Why were they the greatest experiences? Because there were no guides, and often times many times, there also wasn't support. Even organizations that were supposedly designed for support would tell me to get a job. I didn't find it as easy as that and had to figure most of it out on my own.

In 1971, the situation at home got difficult and rough! I had been flunking Algebra, the first time I had ever flunked a class (something not acceptable in my family), and my parents learned I had a girlfriend and was a lesbian. My dad was physically abusive, and on one of the worst nights, I ran away from home. It was February and after seeking counsel of friends, their parents, and receiving guidance from two separate priests and families from church, no one could come up with a solution for me. That night I prayed to God and He answered me and told me to leave for my own safety. I went out my window because my door was locked from the outside. My parents had already planned on putting bars on my window keep me from running away again. I knew I couldn't stay.

I went to Washington DC, as was on the streets at age 17. One night, a woman came up to me and asked me about my situation and I told her. She said she was a prostitute and I could come stay with her and her roommate until I got things figured out. As it turned out, these women were an absolute Godsend! I slept various hours because they were busy with their lifestyle, and often I would leave and visit places around town, such as the zoo and the library. Eventually, my girlfriend wanted me to come live with her and go back to school, but when I tried, the principal said it was not safe for me because my dad kept showing up. There was no place for me to hide from him because he even started looking for me at my girlfriend's home.

I again went back to DC and stayed with the prostitutes. One suggested I go Atlantic City, NJ and get a job waitressing. They put me on a bus and gave me money to for a month's rent and food. I was to get a rental at an ocean side motel and I found a waitress job right away. I was making a good living, although I couldn't sell or serve liquor because I was under 18. I learned about budgeting, and thankfully food was free at the restaurant so I ate every day. Money was good through the summer and I meet transsexuals and transgender people through the bartender. I enjoyed going to drag shows, and went a lot for entertainment. The men kept tabs on me as well, which was very comforting. It wasn't the straight A situation I grew up in academia, but it was 'real time' and I accepted it.

From then on I found my ground and started not only praying to God, but also Mother Earth. I was stable for the first time since being homeless. I figured out a lot of things in that time about myself: I wanted to go back and graduate from high school; I had to give up the idea of being a veterinarian; I wanted to go to college by the ocean; And, I had a dream of getting into massage.

In 1989, I legally changed my name. I had to go before a judge because I was changing my whole name, and not because of divorce. The female judge said no one would ever get access to why I was filing the change, but I truly just wanted and needed a fresh start, and for me that came from changing my name to Beth Jo Sonsé. The judge told me she admired me for doing it!

In the winter of 1998, I was at the height of my massage and personal training career. I published my first book, and had an article featured about me in Massage Magazine. I wanted to give back to the prostitutes that helped me when I was homeless, so I went to work as a property manager of an organization that housed and educated ex-prostitutes, ex-drug dealers, and former abusers. I managed a house and a dorm in exchange for on-site rent and a phone, in Denver, CO. I did maintenance on the house, but I also ended up helping the women if they got in trouble after hours.

I also had a drive to assist in closing two crack houses at the end of the street and to clean up the alley where a lot of crime was happening. I'd been living in the neighborhood and seeing the local high school students going to the crack house. I was coaching volleyball at the school and didn't want to see my students having to deal with the crime and drugs and wanted them shut down. I called the police, with the help of a lesbian who was in the house I managed, every time I saw something.

Emotionally, it all became too much and after 6 months the difficulty and danger that loomed, I knew I had to leave. My therapist was worried about me getting killed by a drug addict, john, or dealer in the houses I was trying to close. She would drive by my house after she got off work to see if my light was still on. I got burnt out and with the exception of a few friends, no one would come over or even call me. And while the organization's administration liked what I was doing, they offered me no support either. I felt the women we were serving had more programs and support than I did. So, one day, I just walked out! My brain had reached beyond its limit. No longer had it become a payback, but rather just an overwhelming experience. And, in that moment, I was homeless again.

Through this experience I met lots of people from various situations. I was exposed to diversity the entire time. I always ran or walked to maintain my physical health, and I learned a lot about money and generosity. There were people who helped that I never would have considered, and other who 'should have' who didn't. I met a lot of people wherever I went. And God (whom I now call Spirit), Mother Earth, and the Holy Spirit (who always kept joy in my life) were constantly there for me when I felt alone and was in scary times. I did it. I survived homelessness twice and learned through them the very basics of life and what really matters to me!

"Today more than 20 scientifically controlled studies of EMDR have proven its effectiveness in the treatment of traumatic and other disturbing life experiences."

Francine Shapiro

"The good life is the journey not just the destination".

Carl Rogers, Psychotherapist

This a variation on a story I encountered in massage school when our class was studying Active Listening from Carl Rogers. I have made adaptations through my years, but it is this:

"There are three boats that start on a shore in America, heading towards Hawaii on the same date. One boat has all the top notch nautical equipment. Everything is planned out to the maximum. It has the right steering for the fastest trip, the best sails, and food is totally taken care of for the amount of time the first boat will take to get to Hawaii. The ship is the best ship supplied for the trip.

On the third boat, the crew is totally aware of the sun, moon, and stars to navigate the way and are able to assess what to do based on changes in the wind or waves. The men take time to put down the anchor and swim with the sharks, dolphins, and whales. They plan the basics in regards to food and plan on catching fish of all kinds on their trip. They take along libations because they're going to get to Hawaii and have a good time getting there. Their boat is strong and they have all the sails they need.

Then there's the second boat. The second boat is called 'Spirit'. It is selected based on the best natural wood and handmade sails from a local owner in a community where all the men were selected based on their experiences. All the men are friends and well qualified for the trip. They have nautical equipment and supplies for the trip, and while they plan to fish, they had plenty of supplies just in case of trouble on the seas. The men were also in relationship with the natural forces, but wanted a solid foundation of equipment for a fun and safe trip."
I told this story to my first therapist, and when I finished she asked, "Who got their first?"
My response: They all got to Hawaii!

While I feel the spiritual boat gets there first- the most important thing is that all got there. The rest isn't important. Who do you think got there first and why? This open ended question, and others like it, are what I learned to ask other people. It helps me and others to think and step outside the box, something I didn't do much of before therapy.

ACTIVE LISTENING IN A THERAPEUTIC SETTING

So some of the techniques I learned as far as listening in a professional setting for Massage Therapy were:

Communication skills, especially speaking

Non-Verbal Communication

Active Listening

These were college level courses and the predominate one was learning how to speak in front of a classroom full of students. The objective was that by the end of a 50 minute class, I was able to keep their attention, teach subject matter well enough that the students could retain it for tests, and get the students to write assignments.

The non-verbal communication class taught me to pay attention to non-verbal cues from students. I found it true that 'actions speak louder than words' and body language can even say much more that the actual words being said. This assisted me in preventing some behavior problems because I could see, as well as hear what a student's thoughts and expressions were and what they actually were trying to come across to say.

Both classes provided helpful while teaching a class and while I was coaching a sport (track & field, volleyball & softball), but today, I also use the skills in my massage therapy, and my personal life. Active listening is also important as well because it gets you engaged to listen to what's being said, but to also encourages you to concentrate more. Sometimes we listen to what we think a person is saying, but without clarifying what we think we heard, there's a good chance of misunderstanding. You likely heard what you think was being said, when actually the other person said something entirely different. Some suggestions on being an active listener are:

- Reflect back to a person by paraphrasing what you think you are hearing
- Ask key questions to clarify areas you might not really know what they mean
- Summarize key points regularly to stay on track with the conversation

The non-verbal communication is important as well, so smile and use expressions as the conversation goes along. Consider how you are holding yourself (are your arms open and is your head looking forward towards the speaker)? Do you agree or disagree by nodding your head?

It's important to try to be non-judgmental in an active listening role, but don't agree to things you see differently by nodding your head 'yes' when you actually feel differently. However, defer judgment by not interrupting.

Sometimes, I'll say to a person, as an example of active listening, "Is this what I'm hearing you say?" Or I'll clarify with, "What do you mean when you say….".

I find that active listening helps me professionally in careers I've had as well as in friendships and relationships. It's a never ending creative endeavor for me to keep up with active listening skills and, from my own experiences in conversation where I am the listener, active listening helps a lot with all age groups and people of different ethnicities. People's cultures and languages are very different from each other and using active listening I find I'm able to get more enjoyment out of the conversation. I understand others better and I learn a lot about subjects I had little knowledge.

EMDR – EYE MOVEMENT DESENSITITIZATION & REPROCESSING

This is a technique used by my therapist with me and it helped tremendously with gaining control of my life again after experiencing an assault and rape. I had gone to a concert with a friend and was caught off guard going to my truck when two men attacked me. I felt ashamed that I didn't fight back and felt like I let it happen to me. With EMDR I saw the incident very differently and started gaining some control back over my life. But in November 2013, as I was leaving the back of 2Succeed where I worked, a woman driving in the alley almost ran over me while I was loading thing in my car. I jumped out of the way and ended up hitting my head on the building's electrical box. Both these occurrences created severe PTSD.

I felt like I was out of control, but with EMDR, I created my own version of a remote control- which is just a tool that feels like it puts me back in control of my outcomes. Because I am very tactile, keeping a physical remote control in my pocket really helps me to remember what I've learned, so to this day I actually carry a small remote control to remind me to Pause, Stop, Go Forward, Go Back, and Quickly Go Forward. It helps me in current situations where I might digress on my healing to get to the present, slow down, and reverse or go forward where I can go to another train of thought. Other techniques I use are "getting to my safe place" and "travel on a slow moving train".

I was in regularly therapy but it just exasperated the experiences, so I stopped. These experiences caused me to have great difficulty at work, but I never told anyone about them except therapists. I know if I'd had EMDR soon after the experiences my life would look a lot different now, but it's never too late to heal. I've come to enjoy life more, take myself seriously when it's needed (instead of just brushing things aside because I'm not important enough), and write this book without the PTSD overriding it.

I believe that EMDR would curb the amount of time needed in therapy for people dealing with the same issue over and over again. Of course, having Kseniya as my therapist has affected the love for life I have again! EMDR is also used in sports enhancement, simple types of mental distractions, and, amazingly enough, even effects how I respond with my dog. With EMDR I have learned to calm my thoughts down and feel more emotions, but not feel them as strongly as when the event happened. It also helps me with changing limiting beliefs, abuse, test anxiety, and even going outside and walking with my dog. I feel the passion in my life returning and I definitely feel more engaged than I have ever felt in my life.

Within a therapeutic setting, it helps me when I'm in a conversation with a massage client who is spiraling downward into deep depression. I simply say, "Let's pause", or "Is there something on your mind that's distracting you?" or "how does this feel" when I'm noticing parts of the body being tightened. I'm finding new ways to use EMDR all the time and am grateful to my therapist for her training. This treatment helped me in just months, rather than in years, to be able to recover and get back into my present life!

"The good life is the journey not just the destination".

    Carl Rogers, Psychotherapist

My two favorite books regarding psychiatric issues for me were and are: "Crazy, A Father's Search Through America's Mental Health Madness" by Pete Earley, and "Psychological and Social Aspects of Psychiatric Disability".

In the first book, my understanding of what happened to the father was that he found systems fail individuals. This is my own experience as well. According to Margaret J. Wheatly in her book, "Finding Our Way", systems fail because they don't meet the needs, creativity, or motivations of staff or clients. Systems forget the human factor existing within an organization. It seems that systems strive for a specific set of standards rather than the needs of existing staff and clients, and, they fail to get valuable input from them. As a result, staff don't have the drive and creativity it takes to do their work, and they burnout.

My favorite chapter in the second book is: 'Power, Powerlessness, and Empowerment in Psychotherapy' by John E Mack, Professor of Psychiatry at Cambridge Hospital, Harvard Medical School. This chapter gave me something technical enough to use while I worked with client's at MHCD in the Wellness area, and also it ended up helping me when I performed chair massages at Ft. Logan (a psychiatric ward facility) on the staff. This chapter addresses what happens in the lives of people when we have a male-dominated society (system), the distresses of minority groups, and people victimized by a political system. (I talk more about this later in regards to Tier 1 people as well.)

When I performed chair massages at the MHCD annual conference, this book was so very helpful because I had people coming from out of the country and from different psychiatric facilities. This diverse group, made up of both staff and clients, received massage from me for 15 minute increments from 7am to 3pm. I worked with CEO's, speakers, clients from various places and the general public. Because Mark Canjar ran the conference, I was given a latitude to be able to work freely on people in the whole spectrum of life, except for children. Mark's technique of hands off management was so powerful and empowering for me. The massages were conducted out in the open so people could see who was receiving touch. I was told we would never be able to massage people from all walks of life in the same place- but we did.

During my time at MHCD, a psychiatrist took me aside and he told me several of his colleagues saw noticeable changes in patient aggression as well as them being able to tolerate less of their heavy medications by using the weight equipment (we had a Universal and free weight system) and receiving the chair massages. He wanted to let me know I was making a difference. I also heard this also from a private psychiatrist who met with

MHCD psychiatrists for a support group. I wish at the time I would have done more research to back the observations.

When I was at Boulder College of Massage Therapy I did a research project on the effects of one-hour long massage clients for 6 weeks. The clients were a deaf psychotherapist and an interpreter for the deaf. They each came at the same time for 90 minutes every Friday night to do a 15 minute pre and post data survey and receive an hour massage. When I finished, my physiology instructor told me research was much needed in the field. I was so overextended with working full-time in Denver and commuting to Boulder four nights a week and Saturdays for classes, that I never published the results, but to me it was a phenomenal experience!

I later tried to find two women who were in recovery from breast cancer in order to do research project but I was unsuccessful. Even with help, I couldn't find two willing participants.

My best friend Katie Carr-Anderson and her family.

Intercessory Prayer Warrior, Gladys Drew. Gladys is black and Japanese and receives requests from all over the world, both from churches and individuals, to pray for them.

Emily FitzRandolph and Quinsetta- My spiritual guide who has helped me massage some of the most disadvantaged women. A very close friend, editor of my second book, spiritual mentor and my massage agent who has helped me massage some of the most disadvantaged women; Quinsetta is my second favorite dog and brings comfort to clients at WHI while I perform chair massage. She lets them pet her while they're in the chair!

My neighbor, Delia Gutierrez, and her family. She is a non-traditional healer and we often trade services to heal each other. Other parts of her family reside in Mexico and Florida.

My friend, Betty Round (an astrologer) and her partner, Peggy Gardner. Betty and Peggy are close friends, breast cancer survivors, and massage clients.

My friend Nancy Keene, who helped me and others as a champion for the GLBT Community.

Sara Bartley graduated from the Denver Seminary and was instrumental in getting me to attend Highlands Community Church.

Gail McClelland and her partner, Jennifer. Gail is an internationally ranked massage therapist who got me into massage therapy.

Gail M. and her family- neighbors and friends of mine. When I was running a food bank out of my house I would include her grandchildren for food assistance.

Chapter 7: Non-Traditional Healing Modalities

Delight yourself in the Lord and He will give you the desires of your
heart.

Psalm 37:4

Non-traditional healing modalities include: Massage, Bodywork and
Somatic Therapy which support the Holistic Health Concept.

The first experience I had with massage was with my mother when I was
in grade school. My mother would lie on the couch at night watching
television and she'd have me massage her feet. I'd do it for an hour and it
was wonderful. My mother said I was a natural and told me about Janet
Travell, MD. Janet was President John F. Kennedy's massage therapist
and later went on to write two volumes on Trigger Point Therapy and
Myofascial Release, which I learned about in massage school. So, at the
early age of 7, I knew I wanted to give massages. Throughout my life until
massage school, my friends would have me give them massages and I felt
so complete.

After college where I earned a BS in Physical Education, I went to work at
the Secretary of Health and Human Services. While there I learned that in
Congress, men had a health club with massages, so I went over to the
health club and talked to the massage therapist. He was a physical
therapist professionally and he provided deep tissue massage to the

Senators and Representatives. I was also told the women in Congress did not have a health club or massage services.

After a while working in the government I decided I wanted to get into health care, so I came out West because I heard there was a World-Class massage school in Boulder. By 1988 I was attending the Boulder College of Massage Therapy and it changed my life!

In the Department of Health and Human Services, they created a federally funded workout program. They planned on creating five fitness centers throughout the country, but when taxpayers heard about it, and that it may include massage (which they felt was highly inappropriate because they had sexual connotations associated with it), they closed it down.

When I left there, I volunteered doing massage at Breast Cancer and HIV/AIDS walk/runs. A massage therapist who ran the massage program at the University of Colorado's Health Sciences asked me if I wanted to go to work there and I said yes. That started my career as an Assistant Program Director and Community Service Coordinator. At first, I performed massages on nurses then I attracted a lot of HIV/AIDS clients. Following that, I was asked to massage breast cancer clients, and so I did.

From there came Hospital Based Massage Therapy (HBMT) where I became certified. I worked there 7 years and worked on people from all over the country and world at University Hospital. I also created a massage-a-thon (written about in my first book "Massaging in Times of

Illness: My Experiences with Massaging in Breast Cancer and HIV/AIDS). One aspect of HBMT was massaging in the Bone Marrow Transplant Unit (now it is called Stem Cell Replacement). I also performed chair massage here.

After leaving CUHSC I went to the Jewish Community Center as a personal trainer and massage therapist. Here I worked on a lot of people who are Jewish and also professional athletes. From there I went to the Mental Health Center of Denver at 2Succeed. (I talk more about this in my second book, "Reaching for Recovery and Wellness with Benefits From Massage: Experiences of People with Mental Health Issues"). I was here for 13 years and performed chair massages in a variety of settings for MHCD, 2Succeed (once every week), and I massaged Ft. Logan's staff once every 3 months, on my own. As I massaged, I connected through and to Mother Earth, sending energy through my touch, and down my body and into my feet. I have always had a spiritual connection doing massage.

Then, I needed two total knee replacements from all my activity in my life. Afterwards I started massaging people from the church I went. I ended up buying new equipment to clean the energy from my previous massage table and massage chair. My spiritual life became significantly greater (as I call this Spirit, Mother Earth and Holy Spirit). While my massage style has changed, I still use Integrative, Reflexology and Chair Massage as my main practices, and believe it is the reason I came her on this earth. I knew this very early in my life and it's no coincidence that I found out about Janet Travell, MD so young.

To me, I consider the following to be the Tiers we have in America.

Tier 1: The disempowered class

Tier 2: The middle class

Tier 3: The upper class

I want to reflect on each so we can better understand their roles and beliefs as a part of holistic health.

TIER 1

People of Low Income, Poverty, Homelessness

I believe Tier I people need to work with those who encourage them to attain a sense of autonomy. I believe that people who are low income, in poverty, and homelessness can take care of their health, relationships, finances, spiritual connection and have the ability to heal and create on their own, with support. Support is key, and letting them do for themselves.

For example, I used to work for the Mental Health Center of Denver's 2Succeed. For 4 years, starting with year 1, we ran a small drink sales booth at the Cherry Creek Arts Festival in Denver. I picked some staff to support clients with disabilities or who were low-income to run the booth. Their job was to take festival participants' orders and collect cash. Others go the drink and brought them to the counter. It was a slow process and staff were encouraged to assist transactions, but to let the clients feel like they completed the process by themselves. This was done for 4 hour shifts, 3 shifts a day for three days and was a success. It was a great start and every client showed up to work. That first year, I was there each day with them to provide consistency as they finished up and went back to 2Succeed and told other clients how it went.

After the event we received very good feedback from the woman who supervised all the booths (there were beer booths, food booths, etc.). We did this event 3 more years and we received more responsibility as it progressed. This experience provided the clients more motivation each year to handle finances, work with different ethnicities within 2Succeed, and to view working with staff differently. Being at a large event in a small space with lots of product and money provided them a way to focus on something other than their disability. We all were able to work with people of varying incomes who were there primarily for the arts. It also benefited everyone to be outside and performing an activity – running the drink booth and it created a huge sense of competence.

Everyone who participated, including the vendors, had a pleasant gathering and event. I believe we found something greater than ourselves that day too. We were able to breathe in more air and people learned they were respected by others for a common good. Whatever you do has a ripple effect, like a rock you throw in a river or the ocean and skips across the water.

In regards to homelessness, I have been proud to contribute to an organization called The Women's Homeless Initiative, (WHI). It is a program where 20-25 women of different ethnicities and abilities meet at a bus stop for WHI and come to one church (one church in Denver each night provides the space for these women). Volunteers from the churches provide enough food for a dinner and it is served to the women, almost like eating at a diner. I doubt most of these women have ever eaten in a safe, respectful place such as this, and they have time to relate to each for an entire evening until the morning, where they are given a paper bag of food when they leave. Smoke breaks are provided and a volunteer or two spend the night to maintain a sense of safety for each and all women.

The women learn to be in relationship with other homeless women who have come from a variety of backgrounds. The spiritual connection is huge whether anyone realizes it or not, even though no specific religious practice occurs, other than sometimes prayer. I think the women feel a sense of competence to stay safe, receive a healthy meal, and take part in each night's activities. However, this is very hard to see only being there once a month- it may be months if I ever see her again.

These events provide women the ability to learn self-control in relation to other people's space and belongings. I've also seen mothers who volunteered and brought children initially keep a close eye on them and then as time passes, they become more relaxed and trusting of the women around their children. This experience teaches the intrinsic rewards of respect for boundaries. The volunteers, usually in another tier, respect the women and provide support, only intervening when someone challenges the rules.

I provide 10 minute chair massages at one church a month to contribute in my own way. Many of the women probably have never received safe touch. Many of the women are also probably touch deprived except in less than desirable circumstances. (However, I have found some women who had at one time made a good living, were in families, and had received full massage therapy.) Even though I am giving back, some clients in the other two tier groups, have felt uncomfortable that I've massaged homeless women, and some have even told me I should stop.

Boundaries are such an important aspect of health, especially for women. Often their health has been jeopardized by another being in their space. In WHI, women can learn to move into HUD apartments, or into other housing solutions. Women begin to learn trust and keep money on them or even in their cot space without concern of it being stolen. This could be due in part to good supervision, which teaches them others are looking out for them, thus building new relationships.

One night, the homeless women at Corona all gave me thank you cards and drew on them. I felt so much support from them and they never knew it. I kept all the cards. During my first knee replacement surgery, I stayed at Porter Hospital and I went in my room after the surgery and put all their cards around my portable food table. Every time I had the table wheeled over for me to eat I looked at them. The Porter staff asked about the cards and I told them they came from the women at the Women's Homeless Initiative. It's that ripple effect!

On my business card I have a quote one of the woman gave that says, "Take me away from it all, Jo". People don't understand that even a 10 minute chair massage is a mind, body, and spirit thing. For just 10 minutes these women are where they are, without judgement. It means a lot to us both.

It seems that what one person does affects others and you just can't even imagine the impact when it's all done. For example, seniors have lost the Meals on Wheels program. So, AARP and Chase Bank are now setting up a food bank for them. People are gathering over the weekend to put food together into meals and provide them to low-income, and/or homeless seniors. Seniors, due to mobility issues, have a hard time getting to food banks. They are limited not just in income, but the ability to make income as well. Food is a primary and survival need. The inability to get it can create additional issues such as lack of self-esteem and self-confidence. Add to this that they may be dealing with pain, disease and mobility issues, work is just not an option. Instead of judging, people should find ways to connect to elders in our communities who are struggling and learn their stories.

I find that a lot of people know me because of the work I do, and just because I don't work in those setting anymore doesn't mean I don't talk to people I recognize when I see them. I often hear, "You probably don't remember me," but I do. One young man said, "I bet you don't have my poems I gave you," but in fact I still do and have shared them with other health care professionals who marvel and his poems.

I had the pleasure of going to the Minimum Security Prison in Colorado Springs to provide chair massages for a day. One man I massaged told me that when he was a little boy he misbehaved and his father was very upset with him. To teach his son a lesson, he grabbed him, a gun, and his puppy and took them into the bathroom. The father put the puppy in the bathtub and shot him and told his son he would do the same to him if he misbehaved again. The man started crying while he the story and said he knew that didn't excuse his behaviors that put him in prison. Wanting to make amends, he started a rehab program in prison and started turning his life around. He was ready for a new life, if it was so deemed.

This man started out in relationships that would lead him into a life of crime. And now, while in prison, with the help of the rehab program, he learned about own behaviors and how to relate to other people differently. In prison he learned how to budget, worked out and had three meals a day. He kept his health up and accepted a chair massage from me. He carried a cross on a chain around his neck, but we didn't get into the spiritual aspect of his life.

This man is a living, breathing organism, and what he did affected himself and others. He had an impact on me in the positive and I really believe his life was leading him to feel more complete. This black man was changing a life that started violently and was now turning himself around in a diverse setting – prison life.

Bless them all and may we keep blessing them for being here!

TIER 2

People from the Middle Class

A deaf woman working at the IRS where I was the Health Improvement Program coordinator came up to me and asked me if I would coach her deaf women's team at West High School. Since I was a volleyball referee and co-coach of a women's team, I said yes. I asked a friend of mine who is an interpreter for the deaf if she would teach me basic sports sign language and some social language.

It was 1985 and I showed up twice a week to coach the women's team. We started with the basics and built up over the season to improve their skills. During that time something happened that was one of the most life changing experiences in regards to my social skills. A woman who was deaf, and a teacher at West High, could read lips and told me my facial skills weren't congruent with what I was saying! She set aside some time to teach me what she meant. Basically, I learned that when I was happy, being funny, upset, or frustrated, I had the exact same look on my face. So, she taught me to use my eyes, forehead, and mouth to express my emotions. It was totally amazing! I was also told not to use sarcasm because it wasn't understood and I wouldn't explain it. I had several years with them to work on myself and my expressions!

In 1997 our team hosted the Deaf Women's Regionals. Teams from other states came to play in our tournament and I was selected to be one of two referees. I was amazed that everyone in the community – mothers with babies in strollers, elders from the community, men and women who were friends, neighbors and family- came in support of the teams. The place was packed all weekend long even though it was a paid event. I had never seen people charged for a volleyball tournament but that is how they paid for school rental, food, etc.). The support for these women's teams was phenomenal. It was also funny that the event was totally quiet. It was difficult to both referee and coach and not talk because they couldn't hear me or the whistle.

After the tournament, our women's team went to Nationals. There was both a competitive tournament and a recreational one. The team I coached went to recreational, but sadly I didn't go because I really didn't know social language to be able to communicate. They went and the woman who asked me to coach ended up coaching them, and the team won the recreational division! These women knew the intrinsic rewards of playing. It wasn't my effort that made them be able to go and play competitive recreational volleyball. They learned it themselves and were able to go without me, play and win.

One day, after the tournament, we were practicing and a girl from the deaf high school in Colorado Springs came to practice with us. She was very good and I learned she was practicing to try out for the National Deaf Women's USA Team. I later heard she was selected for the Olympics in Australia!

The health of the deaf community is very strong and supportive of each other and activities that went on in Denver. Relationships were key. During the tournaments I never saw one person overweight and it was mind boggling. I came to know a lot of people that worked at the IRS and they were deaf! They had jobs and careers I didn't even know existed until they told me. Spiritually, I learned to be respectful of what I say and do with diverse groups after these experiences. It made me very 'careful and mindful' of my place in Denver and with people from anywhere in the world.

TIER 3

People from the Upper Class

"We must learn to offer the World a way to approach that which honors both ego's desire to be holy and the soul's true delight at getting to be all too human."

Jacqueline Small

First, I want to acknowledge that this tier is about people who are rich in the way they go about their lives. The pictures of people I chose for this book are who I consider rich people. They take their health, their relationships, finances and spirituality seriously and they do so with gratitude and love. Their careers run the gamut of doctor to a person on disability who ministers to people around the world in prayer requests. BLESS THEM ALL.

The woman I admire the most is Jean Watson, Ph.D. who created the Center for Human Caring at Colorado University's Health Science Center in the School of Nursing. When I first came to the Center for Human Caring Wellness Center I was a licensed massage therapist in Denver, CO. I've always been well-read and curious so I wanted to know about this woman. The Acting Dean in the School of Nursing gave me two copies of Jean Watson's book and I read them voraciously. They were phenomenal and inspiring, so inspiring that I carry a trinket on my key chain that says "Inspire", which reminds me of Jean every time I look at it.

First of all "The Center for Human Caring" sounds wonderful, doesn't it? It absolutely resonates with me. She is always looking for health care funding for the Center, is humble and has multitudes of relationships, besides her own family. Mother Earth brought me to her program where I ended up taking on Assistant Wellness Program Manager and Community Service Coordinator. Today I am still inspired by her even though I'm not in that setting anymore.

Another "rich" woman is Nancy Keene! There's too much to say about this humble woman. Since the 60's she has been the Mother of the Lesbian, Gay, Bisexual, and Transgender community. Nancy was my mentor into the Spiritual LGBT Soul Force Movement. We even got locked up in the same section of a paddy bus for criminals because we were in a non-violent protest with other LGBTs. Nancy was probably at every Gay Pride Event, usually in a vehicle showering everyone with love and support! She monitored her health well and after the end of her marriage she was able to sustain herself in a career. She was a steady PFLAG (Parents and Friends of Lesbians and Gays) Mother, and is valuable beyond words. I was always welcomed to be with her in any group, with her family, and extended family. As Nancy aged into her 80s her family encouraged me to let go of her and they would care for her! It was never anything I meant to have happen, but it was her families wish.

Michelle, who was a nurse, was my partner for five years in the 1990's. When I met her the first time, she was pretty distant, but I immediately fell in love with her. She had a career in Seattle but was in Denver because her parents had both fallen ill and wanted to remain in their home until they passed away, so she came to take full care of them. Her mother had cancer and her father had lung disease, and she cared for them an entire year until they passed, her father first, then her mother. Caretaking had taken its toll on Michelle and I admired her then and still do now. Michelle became a home health nurse and I the Assistant Wellness Program Manager at CU Center for Human Caring.

I remember our first date: Michelle's sister had a newborn baby and she and her husband wanted a night out, so Michelle and I babysat. I was embraced totally by Michelle's entire family. One time I was working for

Epicurean Catering on New Year's Eve for John Elway's Dealerships. He invited all his staff and we catered the party in a plane hanger that used to be used by Lowry Air Force Base. The floor was unforgiving. The evening ended and four of us were singled out to stay late and finish a last project. The supervisor handed each of us a box with 4 tall glasses for beer, each with John Elway's signature. When I got home I saved them and later gave them to Michelle's brother-in-law. His face lit up, but did I get in trouble with his wife and Michelle! Michelle was a brave breast cancer survivor while we were together. She was very brave! I think because Michelle took so good care of herself- health wise, financially and her love of family- I think that's why she caught it so early and fought it so bravely.

Lastly, of the women, I want to thank my therapist, Kseniya Bahktin. She brought me EMDR. I admire that she is from Russian and left her career as a pediatrician there to bring her family to the United States. In everything she did- the way she talked with me, the way she moved her chair close to me to do EMDR- everything she did was so gentle. I am still her client today because of this. She is with me in spirit whenever I write as I always imagine I'm writing to her. This is a quality of an INFJ, which I am, meaning I am a healer, counselor and a minister. Kseniya always shares herbal tea with me before the session. I am certain her health is very good. And financially, in her relationships, and spiritually she reminds me of Ghandi in woman form, but as a counselor in Denver CO, far from Russia.

As far as men go, John Gribben, MS was my Director at the Center for Human Caring Wellness Center. He held onto people. And he was so gentle, in great shape, yet good in management. As a male mentor sometimes I would think about doing research in the hospital in massage therapy and he told me no! I was too valuable to him and I was the most creative person he'd ever met. Oh my gosh, he really said that to me! He let me create, create, create and was very comfortable around women because all his siblings were girls. He wrote the most eloquent referral for me I have ever gotten. And he knew I would read it and cherish what he wrote, because he wrote it!

Carl Clark, Psy.D, CEO of the Mental Health Center of Denver was an outstanding CEO. Even as CEO, he still sees clients weekly, and this isn't known by many. I don't think he understood me and he had moments were it seemed like he tried. I could identify with him because on the weekend he was a maniac sports enthusiast. I saw pictures of him kayaking. I also was a maniac athlete. I could also identify with myself performing chair massages once a week for the entire 13 years I was at MHCD. But once a year I did maniac chair massages from 7am – 3pm at MHCD's Annual Conference. I did this for 4 years under Mark Canjar! They were 15 minutes each, one right after another. Carl asked me from across the aisle if my hands every got tired and I said no, however, I would get hungry, and there was plenty of food at the conference to keep me working. He just walked away and I know he didn't get it! Most people don't get it. For me, it's about touching people of all incomes, lifestyles, health care issues, and spiritual beliefs all in one day and never letting touch from one energy go into another's because I am connected to Mother Earth and she takes everyone's energy and does what she will with it!

Lastly is Pastor Robb. Pastor Robb heads the Church of the Adventist off Federal Blvd in Denver CO. He came into my life after a year and half of two surgeries for total knee replacements. At his church the congregation would provide meals every other day while I was recovering from surgery at home. Then I started providing meals for mothers and fathers who had newborns and sometimes had another child at home. After awhile I started doing Wednesday prayer circle with him and a woman Deacon. This is when I found spirit, kept mother earth and the holy spirit. (I wouldn't say this to him. I just let Lord crop in). The time came when we had to deal with my being a lesbian and he said I was a sinner, no bones about it. I told him, 'Oh yeah, love the sinner but not the sin'. Then I told him 'I love him as a man but not as the Pastor', no bones about it and I left his church. Today he still refers his family to me for massages and I do love the man, because he can take care of his congregation and because he takes care of himself now.

All of these people have the ability to heal and create in their lives and probably always have been able to do so. The all have their ministries and that's because I've known all of them and seen them in action.

As our world grows more chaotic and unpredictable, leaders are asked questions for which their professional training did not prepare them.

Margaret J. Wheatley

One of the most heartening examples we've encountered in businesses and schools is by agreeing that all behaviors and decisions are based on: 'Take care of yourself; Take care of each other; Take care of this place."

Anonymous quote

The best work experience I've had was when I was the Assistant Wellness Program Director at UCHSC Fitness Facility. My boss, John Gribben, was always telling me to 'Create, Create, Create'. He encouraged me not to get in the traditional medical model where I could research the benefits of massage therapy. Instead, he always encouraged me to stay in our program and he would listen to any ideas and we'd create them together with the other staff, consisting of aerobic and yoga instructors, massage therapists and others. He guided with a soft grip, being certain I wouldn't fail whatever I tried. He always steered me clear of destructive endeavors.

I began my career there with running the front desk and personal training. Gradually, he moved me into a position of independently administering the Fitness Facility's programs in his absence. I also performed massage in the program. Soon we began running successful Mexican food fundraisers, Haircut-a-thons, and made more space available for massage which raised our revenue by over $30,000 in one year. We promoted these events and offerings through newspaper promotion and onsite displays.

From here, John moved me into the first Community Service Coordinator position. It was here I started massage-a-thons for HIV and Breast Cancer patients, a joint event between CU, Project Angel Heart, and Qualife (AIDS and Breast Cancer). I was able to get help from within my massage therapy community and massage schools to always have enough therapists for the events. I also learned the valuable lesson of including everyone in the events with what the cause was, keeping costs down, and getting more participation at the events. We raised $3,000 in a 3 day event only charging $15.00 a massage.

The reason my career was successful was because of the man who guided me, the volunteers, and therapists who participated in endeavor after endeavor for the 7 years I was there. I was able to find people who cared both as a staff person and participant. We were professional and made the events safe with an eye on everyone feeling like it was successful not just for the program but also for the participants. A personal philosophy of mine is to be professional but to always make people feel welcomed no matter the walk of life or diverse perspective.

The second best experience I had as a supervisor was for MHCD's 2Succeed Program at the Cherry Creek Arts Festival. Once again I had a supervisor who supported my creativity and believed in me and my philosophy. We built a trusting relationship together. Her name was Cathy.

At first, the Cherry Creek Arts Festival booth was small (we were just starting out). I worked the whole weekend in the booth having three clients from 2Succeed, (which is a facility for people who have mental health disabilities), work four hour shifts. So, each day there were three shifts over a three day weekend. It was great and the clients were paid minimum wage.

The next 3 years the booth moved closer to the culinary section, which was where the greatest revenue occurred. We were also able to increase the client participation to 30 through the last 2 years. Support is always key. Support financially through income, (clients works more and more while SSI and SSDI slowly go down to help them move into working full-time), support in how to be professional, and support in how to present yourself when selling, were reasons we were so successful year after year. It was so important for everyone's self-esteem to be working at such a high class venue with people happy to see us. There were times we'd see the same customer from year to year. The clients as well as staff marketed our program and the product and it was a beneficial experience for the event itself to have us come each year. It was a win/win situation!

We were also able to work a booth at Pridefest in Denver, CO. I had done a Pridefest booth since 1995 with a friend where she did short astrology readings and I did clothed table massages before a massage chair was affordable for me. With MHCD, our booth offered client art and chair massages. This was a one day event for the first several years then it became a two day event. We had clients volunteer to promote our venue and it was a very diverse experience for them. Eventually the booth expanded from 2Succeed doing the booth to MHCD running the booth and having a family booth too. Volunteers became staff.

I have to admit my income was much higher with MHCD than when I was with CUHSC, but my marketing skills had gotten better and I could reach out to the neighborhood of 2Succeed to let them know about how the program was improving. Eventually I was allowed to go into the neighborhood's Board of Directors and be on the board for 5 years. We delivered event flyers and really build a community in the neighborhood. I firmly believe in community and learned, and am still learning a lot about it from the book "Finding Our Way" by Margaret J. Wheatley. It is a phenomenal book I would recommend on anyone's reading list.

I'd like to end with a poem by Maureen J. Hilliard, SND

"A Parting Blessing"

May you be blessed
With vision
In these shadow times.
May the light invade the darkness.
May it be a soft brilliance,

As bare as candlelight,

Guiding you through

Twilight 'til dawn.

And when the dawn breaks,

May you find yourself

Upon a threshold.

May you enter

And go through,

And may you emerge

Into the dance-

a whole and holy new

dance of grace."

Participating and working in sports and recreation has been a big part of my life. When I was young I was a typical tom boy! The boys were always coming over to our house to get me to play some sport, and I always went. My mom would only let me be out so long then she'd send my dad to get me to come home. They guys thought I was always getting in trouble but I wasn't. In my late 20s, when I moved to my parent's house to help take care of my grandma, my mom started talking about how it was for her growing up in high school, and how girls played sports, for example, girls were only allowed to play half court.

When I went to college I majored in physical education and minored in health. My favorite sports were volleyball and track and field. I learned everything from how to play, how to teach, how to coach, and how to referee or be timer (for track). There were other sports I had to learn how to teach, as well as learning the specifics of educating kindergarten up to high school. I played softball one year in college but mostly played it outside of work.

Sports were where I blossomed. I was, and still am, a pretty quiet person unless I have something to say! But, most of my friends were academia students. I think my biggest accomplishment was getting my National Rating in Volleyball. Outside of work, refereeing, coaching, and playing volleyball were my loves. Don't get me wrong, running was a big asset to me all throughout my life, from childhood until I went to massage school.

In college I took a semester off to train for the U.S. Women's Team in the Pentathalon. If I'd known better then, I would've asked a counselor to coach me or help me understand why physical concerns got in the way, as well as self-esteem. Track and field and volleyball were beautiful sports to watch, and still are. You can catch me watching the Olympics in both sports. Being a military brat, I fit in with physical education classes and could understand the problems my academic friends had. Wherever we went from East to West coast and oversees, they often failed physical education. It was in college, while taking the Education Department's class that I wrote a paper of how physical education could be a win/win for all students. It was a 30 page paper and the professor stopped me and said what I wrote could apply in any class. I saved everything from college- all my papers on ideas I had- from helping girlfriends in modern dance, up to refereeing any sports. I could make really good money for the rest of my life in refereeing, but chose to go to massage school.

It was in volleyball that our instructor, (eventually she became my coach) taught 'classrooms without walls'. It was inspiring and I took it with me when I went to student teach. But the teachers who supervised me didn't understand what I was doing and became quite frustrated with me. I kept going back to Arden Peck, the Professor and teacher/coach in volleyball, and she said I wasn't doing anything wrong. So, I never went into teaching, but went into recreation and there my ideas were allowed because my classes were always full. I taught running and tennis, and refereed the men's and women's league in volleyball. But in recreation, I learned to work with seniors. It opened my eyes to be allowed to play cards, teach macramé and just get into conversations. It was also here that I was taught by an 82 year old woman how to cheat in bridge and other card games! I learned a lot about retirees (both men and women) in the military from helping out in that class.

There were so many adults that influenced me in sports and recreation all around the world. I saw men play field hockey in Tehran, Iran and then again in Washington, DC. Wherever I was in the world, people were playing sports!

Since I graduated from massage school I have worked as the Assistant Wellness Program Director of CU Health Sciences and supervised aerobics instructors, yoga teachers and taught weight training along with doing the Community Service Coordinator for Massage Therapy. After that job, at the Jewish Community Center, I became a personal trainer and massage therapist and worked with professional athletes to the administrators. It was here that I became known for performing pet massages (which I had been trained to do at the Boulder College of Massage Therapy). Mostly Jewish people had me perform pet massage. The next time I would be involved in Alternative Health Care for the Mental Health Center of Denver was 2001. Here I became known for my walking class (which no one had ever had the same experience). I would be here for 13 years.

Chapter 11: Media

In my opinion the media is our checks and balances. Currently the media is under severe scrutiny to take issues and not have their own perspective on the issue. There's never been a better time in my life as of right now for people to read and gain a full understanding of what is going on in our country. Whether about a person's humanistic story, a neighborhood, what's happening in different cities, states, regions, or countries, we really only hear about how they affect the white (or grey, as in seniors) society in our country. Why can't we talk about what's happening anymore to our climate, in our White House, with Russia, or North Korea? There are far greater things about this world than the media acknowledges but it doesn't gets people's attention or money. People buy based on what they see on television, newspapers, computers, cell phones, billboards, etc.

I know I fall into what is targeted towards my interests (which are mostly humanitarian). One example that I think about every month, because I perform chair massages at the WHI (Women's Homeless Initiative), is how this teenage girl lived in a school's staircase in New York City. Her mother passed away and shortly after her father passed away, also. She stayed in the same school staircase, went to high school, and graduated. The New York Times heard about her and requested she write a paper on her life. From that, the New York Times enrolled her (with her permission) in an Ivy League School to study Journalism with a full scholarship. They also had her write for the newspaper sometimes. That really caught my attention and ever since I've read the New York Times when I'm in a Starbucks.

I've always been accustomed to watching television news since I was little. Television was a major family event, although music was, and still is my number one attention getter, next to movies. I still go to the movies! I love the total atmosphere. I've used media for marketing as does everyone. Marketing everything happens nowadays.

The media addresses all cultures, all ages, animals, spirituality/religion, politics, art, sports, education, money, comics, crossword puzzles, love stories, painful happenings, and very scary world politics. Some people in media even have the courage to cover subjects we can't even fathom, such as corruption. They do it because of their passion for free speech of all sorts. It's mind boggling when we think about it and what they do. I can't imagine that most people in media don't love what they're doing, as much as we try to say we don't.

There are places where people don't have media, and our media could cover those stories, but often don't. I feel the media doesn't cover issues around what happens to food that is supposed to go to certain countries and it doesn't get there because it is intercepted. We are trying to address hunger, but because of politics and/or crime, the food isn't getting to those who need it. So, it appears that we don't care about starving people, but the truth is, we do care, the media just doesn't cover it, nor do they address why it's not getting to its intended target.

No one will convince me that the media is not our checks and balances on every issue conceivable.

"Life is NOT practice; it's the real thing!"
Jo Sonsè'

I worked in Washington, DC in the late 80s and early 90s, as the Secretary of Health and Human Services Executive Secretariat. I worked on the latest stand-up computer with a hard drive. I took all the data in the program and merged it all into files and other documents to move a four person office into just me! Believe me, I had a hard time dealing with both data entry and laying off the three people whose job I took. The age of computers was taking the place of peoples' jobs. Amazingly enough the jobs I replaced were those of three black women.

While I was there I used to go on a run around the Washington DC Mall. One night after work a co-worker and I decided to run from work to Georgetown and into Arlington, VA and back because I was training for a marathon. It was beautiful and amazing and gave me a different perspective of DC. Well one day my boss needed a document taken directly to a conference Ronald Reagan was getting ready to speak at, and fast! Because he knew I ran, he asked me to run directly across the Mall and straight to one of the Hotels where the conference was and hand deliver it to him. It really wasn't a request as much as it was direction I had to do. So, I ran over to the conference, the Secret Service let me in no questions asked and, in my shorts, t-shirt, and sneakers, I handed the document directly to Reagan.

I read Doris Lessing's "Short Stories", and remember specifically a story about a homeless woman. One day I brought in a paper bag and drew a woman's face on it. On the top I wrote, "This is a homeless woman! It could be you!" No one made me take it off the desk and I left it there for a week. Another time I was asked to cover phones and the Secretary of Labor called and started swearing about not getting in touch, etc. I told her, "No one swears at me!" and hung up. Oh, baby, did I hear about that!

Eventually, the Director of the Executive Secretariat asked me to go get my Master's in computers and I told him I was leaving within three months to go west and work in health care. On my last day, the Secretary of HHS gave me a picture of her signed: "To the Thorn in My Back".) I threw it away, and moved west, just as I said I would, and have been working in the health care field since- some traditional and some non-traditional.

Now, for politics in holistic health through diversity. Ever since the Inauguration in February of 2017 there's been a slow burning fire going across the country. People slowly but surely are telling their stories in newspapers. I read about them in the New York Times. Right now health care is the big issue and people with disabilities (in wheelchairs even), are sitting outside Senators' offices. People are banding together in non-violent protests all over the world and they're not stopping, no matter what physical actions are taken against them. The fire is growing and sustaining. What does the White House, the Department Secretaries, and Congress waiting for? The fire is still growing. Individuals are taking themselves seriously and taking the ACA Health Care issue seriously. Supposedly, it was going to get rushed through but with the help of the media and people on social media, they're not going to let the Senate put the fire out easily! People have come out of the woodwork.

In college I studied "Classrooms without Walls" and used it Elementary School while I substitute taught. One time, a Professor in Education at Salisbury University was to sit in on the teacher I was subbing for and he stayed while I taught. Afterward he said if I ever wanted to get my Elementary School Teaching Degree, he would make sure I got a full scholarship. But, instead, I have used this in my Health Care Profession which I learned from Arden Peck, a Professor in Physical Education. I would love to also see it take place in Congress in a Summit!

Did you know there have been Summits on Travel and Tourism in 6/2017? The Congressional leaders had a Summit in 4/2017 on business travel with various agencies and people. Did you know travel in the United States has decreased and travel agencies are having to close their doors? People don't want to come to the United States for fear of not being let in, or because if let in, even if living here, have been sent back to where they originally came from.

Politicians have put walls between themselves and their public. There was also a teen summit in 7/2016 that was held at different Planned Parenthood Centers. It was a phenomenal success, but it didn't involve politicians. It was peer teenagers running it!

But we need a Summit of the People with Politicians, Secretaries of Departments in DC, and in The White House, as well as other invested people. I'm not certain how it would work, but I know we need politicians to be open, in an open space, like Schools without Walls. In Schools without Walls, some of the guidelines are: be, respectful, no bullying, listen and be patient, and be partners with other people.

Our Secretary of Education took her first act by cutting funding for people with disabilities in the school systems! I worked with adults with disabilities for 13 years and in the organization I worked in, they also have a child and family center. I don't like the 13 years I worked in the field (and the child and family program) to be discounted by a simple push of a computer button to cut funding. I know when I was there I saw power exerted over other Congressional members, in really unethical ways. When one member comes to power and has a problem with another member, they can do really stupid, and downright mean things, to make their point.

Chapter 13: Stability in our Cultures Today and in Future Visions

Our leaders in the United States of America are not titles. They are people chosen to represent the people, issue, concern and ideology of trust (with a capital T) and sense of duty (with a capital D) for the positions they hold. They are not to only represent certain ones they feel they should address, but rather the ones of the Constitution of the United States of America and the Declaration of Independence. They are not to only represent white, rich men and women but all people, animals, our land, water, and air.

People need to be trusted and not very many people are TRUSTED anymore! What they say and what they do don't match. And, like what Native Americans say 'walk a mile in another person's moccasins'. A friend of mine recently said we have no role models anymore- people we know are looking out for the best interest of all life.

I looked up the definition of TRUST and the one definition that sticks in my mind is: 'a firm belief in the character, strength, confidence or truth of someone or something they have placed their trust in of another human being'. To have stability in our culture today, we've got to reaffirm whether we're deserving of our country's TRUST! A good phrase I heard recently was not just providing 'lip service' but accountability. We can have that again in the leaders in the country once our leaders have looked inside themselves and asked "Am I just providing lip service or am I building TRUST in the life and where our country is headed? Where am I, as a leader, heading this country? How am I performing my duty to as to enlist the TRUST we seem to have lost?"

I think we can find it! Don't give up hope on us. Instead, provide hope within and throughout all of us. I then looked up the definition of DUTY and once again a definition that sticks in my mind is: 'an action or task required by a person's position or occupation that is morally right or an obligation to the life of this country'.

Where are our leaders moral actions, not 'lip service', towards the life of this country? On television one day the Secretary of Defense undermined a Secretary of State because she had no prior service in the military. So, he tried to sabotage her and endanger the country to make her look bad. But an intelligence service member caught up with him before he did damage to our country. The woman told the man, "I am the Secretary of State and I have a sense of DUTY to this country that I represent". Who would you TRUST today in a power struggle from another country to ours? Where's the sense of DUTY amongst our leaders today when there are power struggles from another country to ours?

And, in the instance of Health Care, where is the TRUST in our leaders as a whole? Not, only state by state, but as a whole country? This book is about the value of my perception of holistic health from what my life has been. It's not everyone's. It's just my memoir of my life until now.

So what is our country's memoir of holistic health until now, and where are we going? Plus, what other topics that haven't been a part of my life can be a part of this country's VISION of Holistic Health? It's obvious I probably am one of the most non-violent people I know. So, I can't answer for all aspects of this country I love. And no matter what anyone does or doesn't do, whomever I can and can't trust or feel like they have or haven't be showing their sense of duty, I STILL LOVE THIS COUNTRY! And I'm not going away.

Acknowledgements

I thought years ago that this book would only be a piece of art on the cover. A friend, Ellen, who was a professional artist, did an art work piece with just about every ethnic culture of children and an 80 year old woman. Now, I look at myself and see and imagine at my age being able to have friends, neighbors, and clients from different cultures, all in many of the cities worldwide.

First, I want to thank my editor of my first book, Jill Klunder. Second, I'd like to thank my editor, Kris Jordan for her thoughtful and concise editing skills. I also want to acknowledge the universities I attended. I received my Bachelor's Degree in Physical Education and a minor in Health from Salisbury State University. Then, I went on to receive my Certificate in Massage Therapy from Boulder College of Massage Therapy, and then my Certificate in Hospital Based Massage Therapy from Colorado School of Healing Arts. Finally, I received a culinary Certificate from Johnson and Wales University.

The types of massage I now use from the schools are: Integrative, Myofascial Release, Swedish, Trigger Point, Reflexology, Chelation, Polarity Therapy, and Manual Lymph Drainage (especially for Breast Cancer and HIV/AIDS.) I then went on to obtain a Certificate in "Wellness Recovery Action Plan" and a Certificate in "Pathways to Leadership Process".

Books that motivated me to address some of the chapters were: "God Allows U-Turns", "Care of the Soul", "A Return to Love", "Through a Dog's Eyes", "The Different Drum, Community Making and Peace", "Minding the Body, Mending the Mind", "Trigger Point Therapy, Volumes I & II", "The Bondage Breaker", "The Book of Common Prayer", "Human Anatomy", "The End of Heart Disease", "Medical Physiology", "Crazy, A Father's Search Through America's Mental Health Madness", "Psychological and Social Aspect of Psychiatric Disability", "The Education of Will", "The Silence", "Please Understand Me Volume I & II", "Finding Our Way", "Revolution of World Missions", "Johnson and Wales Culinary Recipes and Culinary Service", "Around the World Cookbook", "Alternative Medicine", Doris Lessing's "Short Stories", and the SOFA writer's Guide "Streamlining Your Writing Tasks".

Massage therapists, psychotherapists, primary care physicians, friends, neighbors, former colleagues and people I met traveling around the world (starting as a military brat) were instrumental in making people, animals, and nature my primary connection to life.

Thanks to all the people who provided their pictures for my book! They remind me of all the types of families and individuals from all walks of my life. I hope they do the same for you. It's amazing that I can say I know these people. I especially want to thank those on the cover: TJ Carlson, Career Consultant; Anju Visweswaraiah, MD and their family. TJ and Anju are massage clients of mine. I chose them because they represent to me the best definition of a holistic family.

A politician who served some 14 years ago, is Senator Tammy Baldwin of Wisconsin. When I first met her, I was the event coordinator for the Metropolitan Community Church (MCC) and she came to speak about running for the House of Representatives in Wisconsin. Now she is their Senator and many of her speeches can be found on YouTube. I admire her for running in a Republican State as an out lesbian and she is part of the reason I wrote the chapter on politics.

Pets have been a huge part in all aspects of my life. Buddy, my tabby, of 16 years, Rusty (my Beagle) was the most gregarious. And, I never thought I'd love another dog like that, and believe me there are no similarities between Rusty, Berry, and Diamond. Berry came with a name from Raspberries, Blueberries, and Strawberries. He was a Blue Heeler, Boxer, Pit Bull mix. After him, I got Diamond, a Border Collie and Labrador mix, at 12 weeks. He had a white light surrounding him and I feel his spiritual love everywhere I go and especially when I'm home!